THE MAGIC OF KEW

KEW GARDENS is one of Britain's most enchanting places. Every year over a million visitors wander, explore and relax there, seeking inspiration, or knowledge, from the enormous variety of plants and trees, enjoying the architectural curiosities or absorbing the beauty and quietness. James Bartholomew has captured Kew's peculiar magic in this album of outstanding black-and-white photographs, published in association with the Royal Botanic Gardens. Through some one hundred sensitive, beautifully composed images, Kew, and the gardens at Wakehurst Place in Sussex, are shown in all seasons, in different lights, from near and distant perspectives, revealing the less well-known corners as well as the more famous, such as the Temperate House and the Pagoda. Surprisingly, this is the first photographic portrait of the Gardens and it now has a particular significance because the pictures were taken before the storm which caused so much devastation in October 1987.

JAMES BARTHOLOMEW

THE MAGIC OF
KEW

THE HERBERT PRESS
in association with
THE ROYAL BOTANIC GARDENS, KEW

ROYAL
BOTANIC
GARDENS
KEW

First published in Great Britain 1988 by
The Herbert Press Ltd, 46 Northchurch Road, London N1 4EJ
in association with the Royal Botanic Gardens, Kew

Designed by Pauline Harrison

Printed and bound in Great Britain by Butler & Tanner, Frome, Somerset

British Library Cataloguing in Publication Data:

Bartholomew, James
    The magic of Kew.
    1. Royal Botanic Gardens (Kew)—
Pictorial works
    I. Title   II. Royal Botanic Gardens (Kew)
    580'.74'442195   QK73.G72R6/

ISBN 0–906969–83–2
ISBN 0–906969–82–4 Pbk

CONTENTS

To Linda

FOREWORD

It gives me great pleasure to introduce James Bartholomew's portfolio of photographs of Kew Gardens and Wakehurst Place. It is an interesting and unusual book for a variety of reasons. Astonishingly, it is the first book of photographs of Kew taken by a single photographer. That these photographs are in black-and-white may initially also cause some surprise but of course many of today's leading photographers do prefer black-and-white, and this medium is particularly suited to James Bartholomew's vision.

He does not see the gardens through the eyes of either a botanist or a casual visitor. Those of us who are privileged to work here know Kew to be a scientific research centre, albeit a beautiful one, devoted to the study of plants and horticulture. Many of our visitors, however, think of us only as a great garden, containing a remarkable collection of historical buildings, whose architecture varies from the idiosyncrasy of the Pagoda and the Ruined Arch to the severely functional lines of the Princess of Wales Conservatory. James Bartholomew, in contrast, is more interested in the patterns made by the juxtaposition of buildings and plants and by the chance association of objects connected with life in a major garden. Seen together these photographs encapsulate, for all users of the gardens, a lot of the fascination and magic to be found in our combined 700 acres at Kew and Wakehurst Place (our satellite garden in Sussex).

This book now has, sadly, a further value in that it is an historical record. Following the storm of October 1987 the landscape at both Kew and Wakehurst Place has changed and certain of the views in the book contain trees which were lost. I am grateful, therefore, to James Bartholomew for not only a beautiful portrait of our gardens but also for making us all, botanist and layman alike, more aware of some of Kew's secret, but for the most part public, places.

PROFESSOR E. A. BELL
Director of the Royal Botanic Gardens, Kew

ACKNOWLEDGEMENTS

Of the many people who helped me in one way or another with this project, several must not go unmentioned. At Kew, thank you to Elaine French, Tony Schilling, Michael King and especially Brinsley Burbidge. Thanks to David Herbert and Julia MacKenzie for producing this book and thank you to John Monroe and Pete Turner for giving me the idea of putting the photos into book format. But most of all a large thank you goes to my wife Linda, without whose support and kind patience this book would not have come about.

INTRODUCTION

THE ROYAL BOTANIC GARDENS at Kew, in Surrey, is both a living laboratory for scientists and a public pleasure garden. To most people, however, they are affectionately known as Kew Gardens. Unlike many modern botanical gardens, Kew is not simply a huge plant collection; there are many buildings of great historical importance. The 300-acre/120-hectare gardens containing a plethora of plants, both outside and under glass, are so extensive that it is impossible for casual visitors to do more than glance at the obvious highlights. For the gardens to be known in any sort of depth requires repeated visits throughout the seasons.

James Bartholomew, a young Scottish-American who has lived on both sides of the Atlantic, was captivated by his first visit to Kew Gardens in the spring of 1984. This was within weeks of returning to Britain after spending the period 1979–84 in the U.S.A. Since then he has paid repeated visits and gradually built up a large portfolio of photographic images. In 1986 many of his Kew prints were on view in two one-man exhibitions at major London galleries. In this book he provides a personal choice of glimpses around both Kew and Wakehurst Place in Sussex, the satellite garden of Kew. Wakehurst has a more varied topography than Kew and a higher rainfall, which allows a wider range of trees and shrubs – notably rhododendrons – to flourish.

Most visitors to these gardens will choose to record what they see on colour film. James, however, prefers to work in monochrome which he regards as the classical approach to photography. By producing black-and-white prints he has complete control from start to finish; an essential factor for achieving the artistic and aesthetic effect he desires. In James's own words: 'I love the thrill of discovering a picture. Although I enjoy darkroom work – having studied fine art printing in the States – it is being outside with a camera and selecting the image in the viewfinder, that gives me the greatest satisfaction. I compose the image in the camera, not in the darkroom. For this reason,

I always print from the complete negative area.' The majority of photographs in this book were taken either on 5 × 4 inch or on 6 × 9 cm negative film.

James's controlled approach to photography – using a large-format camera on a tripod – is the antithesis of the candid approach to documentary photography which, by using multiple exposures of events, seeks to capture fleeting moments of interaction between people and their surroundings. It takes him time to set up his camera and compose the picture, so there are few people in his photographs. They are occasionally used for scale, such as the pair of tiny figures seated on the lawn outside the east door of the Temperate House in Plate No. 55; they appear low down in the centre of the frame where they also contribute an element of the composition. For the most part, however, he has chosen the less transitory aspects of the gardens, the solid structures and mature trees, and treated them as 'still life' images. The pictures will thus stand the test of time.

When I first saw James's prints, I was surprised and intrigued to find not a single floral study among them. This exclusion was another deliberate decision and, I might say, a bold one; after all, the most obvious subjects to photograph in a botanical garden are flowers, but like the figures, they are relatively ephemeral. Larger plants such as palms and trees have attracted James's perceptive eye; but it is the more permanent features – large and small – which are his forte.

Line, form and texture feature repeatedly in James's photographs, both in exterior views and details of interiors. His pictures taken inside the original 1848 Palm House at Kew now have an historical interest, for in 1985 the house was partially dismantled prior to its restoration. I have visited and photographed at Kew and at Wakehurst many times in recent years, so I can appreciate how successfully James has sought out the more remote, rarely visited corners of these renowned gardens. With this portfolio gathered together over a three-year period, James gives us intimate glimpses of Kew and Wakehurst, mostly taken early or late in the day, outside the times of normal public access.

Among these secret cameos taken at Kew those which have particularly caught my eye are the circular mirror reflecting the new Alpine House (Plate No. 44), the collar of snow on the statue in the Queen's Garden (Plate No. 12) and the cart taken in the snow (Plate No. 45), once used by gardeners to transport plants within the gardens.

In complete contrast, I also find attractive the interior of the dining room in the Elizabethan mansion at Wakehurst Place, showing the fireplace with the pair of monks (Plate No. 82), and the beech growing around a sandstone outcrop in Rock Walk (Plate No. 96). My botanical eye coupled with my delight in natural design draws me towards the studies showing the whorled branches of a young Norfolk Island Pine (Plate No. 36) and the palm *Brahea edulis* (Plate No. 26), both taken in the Temperate House.

James Bartholomew is an entirely self-taught photographer. He has become an avid follower of the Zone System, devised in 1941 by the late Ansel Adams as a simplified method for analysing the tonal range of the subject. By dividing the range into eleven zones from black to white, Adams provided the photographer with a tool for assessing the tonal range within the field of view, which could be noted and reproduced in the finished print. James's work is thus a form of tonal painting.

All James's photographic studies portray fine detail, achieved by using slow speed (25 ISO and 125 ISO rated at 80) fine-grain films and stopping the lens right down to the smallest aperture to gain the maximum depth of field. To achieve some of his interiors, the exposure had to be as long as ninety seconds.

I have always believed that for photographs – of any subject – to succeed, they must communicate a sense of discovery. Photographs of static subjects such as architectural features, should make us want to discover for ourselves their shapes or textures under different lighting conditions. For me James's portfolio taken at Kew Gardens and Wakehurst Place illustrates the permanent framework of these gardens. Our eyes can linger and delight in shapes, forms and shadows without being distracted by the ephemeral colour of annual or perennial flowers. Here we have the basic skeleton which is seasonally embellished with floral displays for the delight of visitors.

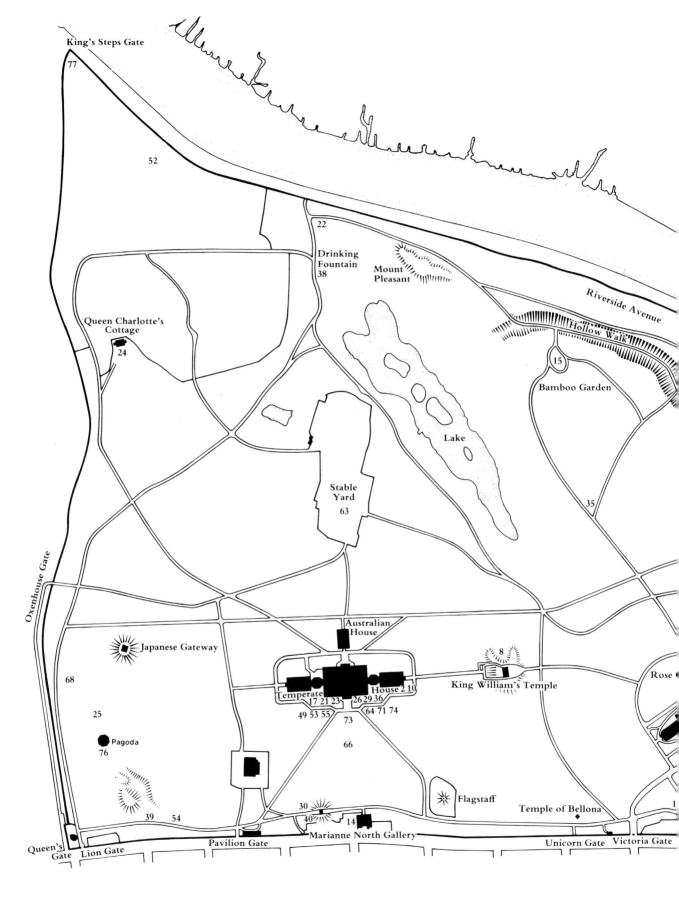

King's Steps Gate

77

52

22

Drinking
Fountain
38

Mount
Pleasant

Riverside Avenue

Hollow Walk

Queen Charlotte's
Cottage

24

15

Bamboo Garden

Lake

Stable
Yard

63

35

Oxenhouse Gate

Australian
House

Japanese Gateway

8

68

King William's Temple

Temperate
17 21 23
49 53 55

26 29 36
64 71 74

House 2 10

Rose

25

73

66

Pagoda
76

Flagstaff

Temple of Bellona

1

30

39   54

40

14

Queen's
Gate   Lion Gate

Pavilion Gate

Marianne North Gallery

Unicorn Gate

Victoria Gate

Kew Gardens

NOTE: The numbers refer to the plate numbers and show, approximately, where the photographs were taken.

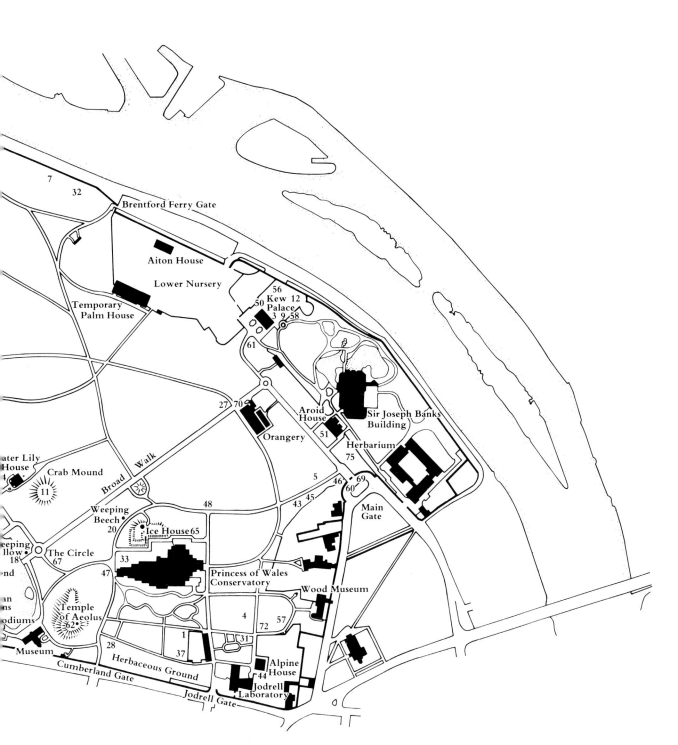

The Gardens of Wakehurst Place

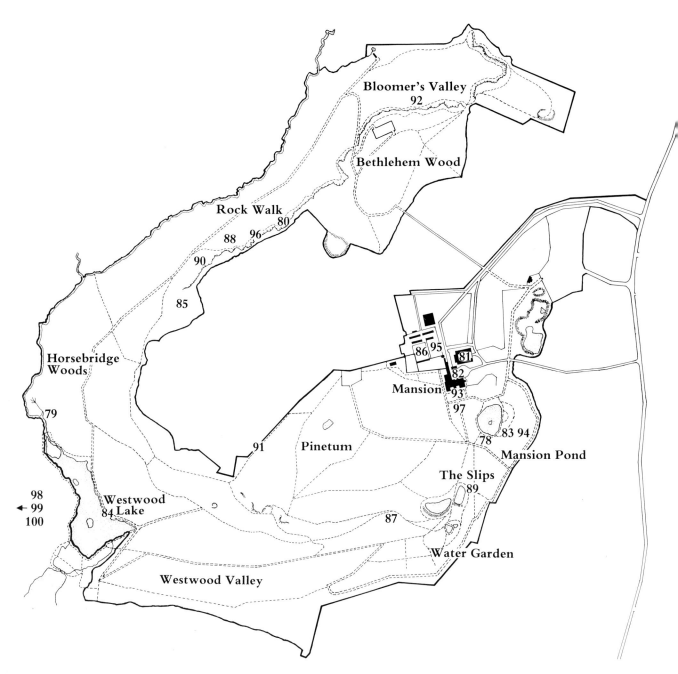

Bloomer's Valley
92

Bethlehem Wood

Rock Walk
80
88 96
90
85

Horsebridge
Woods

79

91 Pinetum

86 95
81
82
Mansion 93
97

83 94
78
Mansion Pond

The Slips
89

98
99
100

Westwood
84 Lake

87

Water Garden

Westwood Valley

THE PLATES

PLATE NO. I: THE DOOR IN THE WALL

PLATE NO. 2: NORTH–WEST STAIRCASE, TEMPERATE HOUSE

PLATE NO. 3: KEW PALACE GARDENS

PLATE NO. 4: *CORTADERIA SELLOANA*, GRASS GARDEN

PLATE NO. 5: *ZELKOVA CARPINIFOLIA*, MAIN GATES

PLATE NO. 6: NORTH WING, PALM HOUSE

PLATE NO. 7: BIRCH TREE, RIVERSIDE AVENUE

23

PLATE NO. 8: KING WILLIAM'S TEMPLE

PLATE NO. 9: HORNBEAMS, QUEEN'S GARDEN

PLATE NO. 11: CRAB MOUND

PLATE NO. 12: STATUE OF WOMAN, QUEEN'S GARDEN

PLATE NO. 13: PALMS IN PALM HOUSE

29

PLATE NO. 14: TEMPERATE HOUSE LODGE

PLATE NO. 15: THE BAMBOO GARDEN

PLATE NO. 16: *CEDRUS DEODARA* AND HOLLY BUSHES

PLATE NO. 17: SOUTH-EAST STAIRCASE, TEMPERATE HOUSE

PLATE NO. 18: SAINT HELENA WILLOW TREE

PLATE NO. 19: CHINESE LIONS

PLATE NO. 20: INSIDE WEEPING BEECH

PLATE NO. 21: OCTAGON, TEMPERATE HOUSE

PLATE NO. 23: STAIRS INSIDE EXHIBITION AREA,
TEMPERATE HOUSE

PLATE NO. 24: QUEEN CHARLOTTE'S COTTAGE

40

LATE NO. 25: *THUJA PLICATA*

PLATE NO. 26: *BRAHEA EDULIS*, TEMPERATE HOUSE

PLATE NO. 27: THE ORANGERY

43

PLATE NO. 28: ROSE PERGOLA AND THE TEMPLE OF AEOLUS

PLATE NO. 29: TOP OF SOUTH-EAST STAIRS, TEMPERATE HOUSE

PLATE NO. 30: SOUTH SIDE OF THE RUINED ARCH

PLATE NO. 31: EUCALYPTUS AND GHOST

PLATE NO. 32: LAWSON CYPRESS, RIVERSIDE AVENUE

PLATE NO. 33: THE PRINCESS OF WALES CONSERVATORY

PLATE NO. 35: DRINKING FOUNTAIN BY THE TULIP TREE

52

PLATE NO. 37: GREENHOUSE OUTSIDE ALPINE YARD

PLATE NO. 38: PINE GROVE, SYON VISTA

PLATE NO. 39: CHINESE PAGODA FROM THE HEATH GARDEN

PLATE NO. 40: ANGEL WITH THE RUINED ARCH

PLATE NO. 41: PALM HOUSE BALCONY

PLATE NO. 42: INDIAN BEAN TREE

PLATE NO. 43: HOLLOW BY FERNERIES

PLATE NO. 44: MIRROR BEHIND THE ALPINE HOUSE

PLATE NO. 45: CART IN SNOW

PLATE NO. 46: BLACK PINE WITH DAFFODILS

PLATE NO. 47: DRY TROPICAL WING, PRINCESS OF WALES CONSERVATORY

PLATE NO. 48: WISTERIA CAGE

PLATE NO. 49: ARCHES, TEMPERATE HOUSE

PLATE NO. 50: *RHAMNUS ALATERNUS ARGENTEOVARIEGATA*,
QUEEN'S GARDEN

PLATE NO. 51: THE AROID HOUSE

PLATE NO. 52: THE CONSERVATION AREA

PLATE NO. 53: STATUE OF DAVID

PLATE NO. 54: LION GATE WALK

PLATE NO. 55: EAST DOOR, TEMPERATE HOUSE

PLATE NO. 56: PAN, QUEEN'S GARDEN

PLATE NO. 57: PRIVATE DOOR

PLATE NO. 58: HORNBEAMS IN WINTER, QUEEN'S GARDEN

PLATE NO. 59: SWAMP CYPRESS, PALM HOUSE POND

PLATE NO. 60: MAIN GATES

LATE NO. 61: *CRATAEGUS MONOGYNA*

PLATE NO. 62: TEMPLE OF AEOLUS

PLATE NO. 63: MANURE IN STABLE YARD

PLATE NO. 64: *RHOPALOSTYLIS BAUERI*, TEMPERATE HOUSE

PLATE NO. 65: THE ICE HOUSE

PLATE NO. 66: TEMPERATE HOUSE THROUGH CEDARS

PLATE NO. 67: GREEK URN, BROAD WALK CIRCLE

PLATE NO. 68: WOODCHIPS NEAR LION GATE

PLATE NO. 69: THROUGH THE MAIN GATES

PLATE NO. 70: DRINKING FOUNTAIN, ORANGERY

PLATE NO. 71: MEDITERRANEAN WING, TEMPERATE HOUSE

PLATE NO. 72: EDWARD VII GATE, DUKE'S GARDEN

PLATE NO. 73: VIEW FROM TEMPERATE HOUSE

PLATE NO. 74: *CIBOTIUM GLAUCUM*, TEMPERATE HOUSE

PLATE NO. 75: BENCH IN SNOW

PLATE NO. 76: STAIRCASE INSIDE THE PAGODA

PLATE NO. 77: THE FARTHEST PLACE

PLATE NO. 79: ASH GROVE BY THE LAKE

PLATE NO. 80: ROCK WALK

PLATE NO. 81: SUNDIAL IN CARRIAGE RING

PLATE NO. 82: MONKS IN DINING ROOM

PLATE NO. 83: BENCH AT 'KODAK CORNER'

PLATE NO. 84: SWAMP CYPRESS, WESTWOOD LAKE

LATE NO. 85: APPROACH TO ROCK WALK

PLATE NO. 87: WESTWOOD VALLEY

PLATE NO. 88: BRIDGE OVER ROCK WALK

PLATE NO. 89: PACKHORSE BRIDGE, WATER GARDEN

PLATE NO. 90: ROOTS AT ROCK WALK

PLATE NO. 91: LAWSON CYPRESS

PLATE NO. 92: WALNUT TREE, BLOOMER'S VALLEY

PLATE NO. 93: INSIDE SOUTH DOOR, WAKEHURST MANSION

PLATE NO. 95: YEW HEDGE AT THE PLEASAUNCE

PLATE NO. 97: STEPS SOUTH OF THE MANSION

PLATE NO. 98: BIRD HIDE, LODER VALLEY

PLATE NO. 99: ARDINGLY RESERVOIR

PLATE NO. 100: PLATT'S BRIDGE, ARDINGLY RESERVOIR

NOTES

KEW

PLATE NO. 1
THE DOOR IN THE WALL

Situated in an obscure corner of lawn near the Rose Pergola, this door is rarely opened by Kew staff although it leads to the Alpine Yard. The *Ercilla volubilis*, behind the *Magnolia delavayi* to the left of the doorway, has been allowed to grow almost completely over the door. On the right of the door is an *Akebia lobata*.

PLATE NO. 2
NORTH-WEST STAIRCASE, TEMPERATE HOUSE

A sign fixed to these stairs requests that only six people use the staircase at one time. Despite this warning, considerably more than six people have made the journey to the walkway above at the same time.

The Australian Tree Fern, *Dicksonia antarctica*, on the right, is related to the giant tree fern which grew 350 million years ago.

PLATE NO. 3
KEW PALACE GARDENS

Seen from the curved stone seat at the end of the Parterre garden, this view shows the back of Kew Palace, and the symmetrical beds that enhance this garden. The statue is a cast of Verrocchio's *Boy with Dolphin*.

PLATE NO. 4
CORTADERIA SELLOANA, GRASS GARDEN

This is one of the largest species of the Graminae, or grass family, found in the Grass Garden, and is indigenous to South America.

This lovely garden includes an interesting display bed of British grasses from different habitats, and a number of larger specimens which show the real ornamental value found in certain members of this family.

PLATE NO. 5
ZELKOVA CARPINIFOLIA, MAIN GATES

Hillier's manual of trees and shrubs calls this 'an elm related tree, that is very long lived and slow growing, with numerous crowded branches'. This tree bears out his notes, having been planted in 1761.

PLATE NO. 6
NORTH WING, PALM HOUSE

A view of the north wing of the Palm House before it was taken down for restoration in 1985. This wing contained Kew's impressive collection of Cycads.

PLATE NO. 7
BIRCH TREE, RIVERSIDE AVENUE

This tree stands close to the Brentford Ferry Gate, the only one of the three original riverside gates still open to the public. The dark background against the snow is a large holly bush.

PLATE NO. 8
KING WILLIAM'S TEMPLE

As the name suggests, William IV was responsible for having this small folly built. It once contained busts of the royal family, but is actually something of a war memorial as the walls bear a set of iron tablets engraved with the names and dates of battles fought by British soldiers during the reign of George III.

PLATE NO. 9
HORNBEAMS, QUEEN'S GARDEN

The two rows of *Carpinus betulus* found next to the Palace were planted as recently as 1965, and have ten rows of *Galanthus nivalis* (snowdrops), underneath.

PLATE NO. 10
SOUTH-EAST CORNER, TEMPERATE HOUSE

The south-east corner of Decimus Burton's Temperate House showing the delicate curves of the iron framework and the graceful sweep of the staircase.

PLATE NO. 11
CRAB MOUND

This small round hillock to the west of the main Broad Walk owes its name to the group of crab-apple trees planted on it. Viewed at close quarters they resemble so many gnarled men walking about. The picture was taken in the summer of 1984 and the foliage has overgrown somewhat since then.

PLATE NO. 12
STATUE OF WOMAN, QUEEN'S GARDEN

One of five carved stone heads that were commissioned in 1734 by Frederick, Prince of Wales. The woman represents a mythological figure, possibly Greek.

PLATE NO. 13
PALMS IN PALM HOUSE

Conditions in the Palm House had to be kept at such heat and humidity levels that in spite of major renovation from 1956–8, the continuing damage to the iron framework was so great that the entire building was closed for renovation in 1984.

PLATE NO. 14
TEMPERATE HOUSE LODGE

Also called Avenue Lodge, this quaint building was designed by William Eden Nesfield in 1866 in the style that came to be known as 'Queen Anne'. The four pedimented dormer windows and especially the massive central chimney stack, make this gate house of an architectural importance out of all proportion to its small size.

PLATE NO. 15
THE BAMBOO GARDEN

Established in the winter of 1891–2 in a dip near the Rhododendron Dell on the site of an old gravel pit, the Bamboo Garden is ideally sited to provide the shelter and root moisture required by these plants.

As bamboos are evergreen, it is especially interesting to see them in winter. They flower at various times of the year.

PLATE NO. 16
CEDRUS DEODARA AND HOLLY BUSHES

Situated behind the semicircle of holly bushes surrounding the Rose Garden behind the Palm House and next to the Water Lily House, this cedar offers two secluded benches in its shade. The surprise is to find another small bench tucked behind the trunk inside the right-hand holly bush.

PLATE NO. 17
SOUTH-EAST STAIRCASE, TEMPERATE HOUSE

A closer view of the south-east stairs (see Plate No. 10) favouring a detail of the spiral stairs themselves. At the bottom, with the leaves covering the banisters, is the Australian Tree Fern (see Plate No. 2).

PLATE NO. 18
SAINT HELENA WILLOW TREE

This mature willow tree is known to have been raised from a cutting of the willow growing over Napoleon's grave. It is found to the north of the Palm House Pond by the Circle.

PLATE NO. 19
CHINESE LIONS

Presented by Sir John Ramsden in 1958, these are copies of the bronze lions which stand outside the

Imperial Palace in Beijing. They weigh almost ten tons each and probably date from the 18th century.

PLATE NO. 20
INSIDE WEEPING BEECH

The branches of this tree form an umbrella that children and adults alike want to investigate. It weeps mostly by itself, except where supported by a guy wire and four crutches.

PLATE NO. 21
OCTAGON, TEMPERATE HOUSE

This is part of the north of the Temperate House, showing one of the two octagons which were built before the main building.

PLATE NO. 22
ALGERIAN OAK, ISLEWORTH FERRY GATE

This *Quercus canariensis* was planted about fifty years ago on a corner where Riverside Avenue meets Boathouse Walk. The photograph was taken in January 1986.

PLATE NO. 23
STAIRS INSIDE EXHIBITION AREA, TEMPERATE HOUSE

A staircase leads from the north wing down into a small circular enclosure which houses an historical display of the Gardens.

There is a narrow and little-known passageway following the air duct on the right to an exit doorway which comes back up to ground level by the Australian House.

PLATE NO. 24
QUEEN CHARLOTTE'S COTTAGE

This thatched, brick building was built on the order of George III for Queen Charlotte in 1772. The actual architect is unknown, although in 1774 *London Magazine* claimed that the Queen designed it herself.

Queen Victoria gave the cottage to the Gardens as a Diamond Jubilee gift, and since its restoration in 1977 it has been open to the public under the auspices of the Department of the Environment.

PLATE NO. 25
THUJA PLICATA

Situated near the Pagoda and next to a weeping holly bush, this interesting tree puts off lateral branches close to ground level. Three of the lowest branches have been removed.

PLATE NO. 26
BRAHEA EDULIS, TEMPERATE HOUSE

This is one of two similar palms found in the north-east corner of the main building. The view is looking down from the walkway, and it has grown considerably since this photograph was taken in 1984.

PLATE NO. 27
THE ORANGERY

Sir William Chamber's Orangery is thought to be the finest architectural work in Kew Gardens, and has an interesting history.

Originally intended to grow oranges, the building was found to be too dark and finally in 1841 the trees were moved to Kensington Palace. The building later housed a number of collections, including a million walking sticks! In 1959, Sir George Taylor tried to grow orange trees there once more but dry rot caused the ceiling to collapse, and the Orangery was closed for repair in 1960. It was reopened to the public in 1971 as a bookshop and orientation area, and has retained this function to the present time.

PLATE NO. 28
ROSE PERGOLA AND THE TEMPLE OF AEOLUS

A wooden trellis adorned with climbing roses bisects the Herbaceous Ground, where thousands of species are grown. At the south end the path splits to go around the Temple of Aeolus.

PLATE NO. 29
TOP OF SOUTH-EAST STAIRS, TEMPERATE HOUSE

Since virtually the whole of the inside of this building is painted white, the only dark part of this photograph is the banister.

PLATE NO. 30
SOUTH SIDE OF THE RUINED ARCH

One of Sir William Chamber's follies, this arch is said to have once formed a causeway over Kew Road for carriages and cattle to come into the grounds.

The masonry carefully distributed around its base is mostly ruins from the arch, and the four doorways recessed into each side that go nowhere reveal the true nature of the arch as a folly.

PLATE NO. 31
EUCALYPTUS AND GHOST

The Tasmanian *Eucalyptus dalrympleana* sheds its bark so quickly that the 'ghost' left sometime in 1984. The lilies planted in the bed behind the tree have names such as 'Resolute', 'Kindly Light' and 'Loveliness'.

PLATE NO. 32
LAWSON CYPRESS, RIVERSIDE AVENUE

This is one of four small cultivated yellow cypress trees (*Chamaecyparis lawsoniana*) planted in Riverside Avenue in 1976. This variety is known as 'President Roosevelt'.

PLATE NO. 33
THE PRINCESS OF WALES CONSERVATORY

The Princess of Wales officially opened the latest greenhouse at Kew on 28 July 1987, although the building had been open to the public since its completion in 1986. These hardy yuccas are on the outside of the semitropical wing, but seem to manage in the English climate.

PLATE NO. 34
BENCH INSIDE HOLLY BUSH

Apart from THE FARTHEST PLACE (Plate No. 77) in the Conservation Area, where visitors are not allowed, this bench competes with THE DOOR IN THE WALL (Plate No. 1) for the least-known spot in Kew Gardens. The secret: it is inside the holly bush nearest to the Water Lily House on the north side of the path around the Rose Garden. Staff claim that a shy old gardener who used to work in this section put the bench behind the trunk to have somewhere to eat his lunch in privacy.

PLATE NO. 35
DRINKING FOUNTAIN BY THE TULIP TREE

Identical to the drinking fountain next to the Orangery, this one is found between the tulip tree and Syon Vista. The Ordnance Survey bench mark cut into the stone shows that the fountain was used as a measured reference point for surveying the Gardens.

PLATE NO. 36
NORFOLK ISLAND PINE

Situated at the north end of the Temperate House, this magnificent tropical Christmas tree (*Araucaria heterophylla*) stands over eight metres high. It is indigenous to Norfolk Island, a tiny South Pacific Island off the east coast of Australia.

PLATE NO. 37
GREENHOUSE OUTSIDE ALPINE YARD

The two sides of this greenhouse display tender plantings from the Alpine Yard. On the left are Spanish Saxifragas and on the right are the Mediterranean Campanulas. They stay in this greenhouse all year except when flowering.

PLATE NO. 38
PINE GROVE, SYON VISTA

Near the clump of small pines at the west end of the Lake is a view from the Isleworth Ferry Gate across the river. The hillock on this side and Mount Pleasant on the other make a small valley which often forms the flight path for birds, such as Canada Geese, who fly in from the river.

This photograph was taken in the early morning in March 1985, and shows the mist that often covers the Gardens at this time of year.

PLATE NO. 39
CHINESE PAGODA FROM THE HEATH GARDEN

Designed by Sir William Chambers, this famous Pagoda was built in the astonishingly short time of six months in 1761–2, and is said to have cost £12,000.

It originally had eighty glass dragons with bells in their mouths, one overhanging each corner of the ten roofs. The dragons were sold in the 1820s to pay George IV's gambling debts and the varnished iron plates which adorned the roofs have been replaced by slate.

The 88-foot high building is the second highest point at Kew, the highest being the Douglas Fir flagpole, which is 225 feet.

PLATE NO. 40
ANGEL WITH THE RUINED ARCH

On the south side of the Ruined Arch are a series of bricked alcoves which were added later. Most of the masonry around the back of the arch is left from the original causeway, which was much taller. This frieze is possibly from a mural above the arches.

PLATE NO. 41
PALM HOUSE BALCONY

Taken in 1984 before the Palm House was disassembled for renovation, this photograph shows the view along the balcony, which is somewhat shorter than the one inside the Temperate House.

PLATE NO. 42
INDIAN BEAN TREE

Surrounding the Rose Garden behind the Palm House is a semicircle of holly hedges punctuated with large round holly bushes. At this place is found *Catalpa bignoniodes*, growing behind the holly.

PLATE NO. 43
HOLLOW BY FERNERIES

The textural blend shown here is a mixture of the trees: *Cedrus atlantica* on the left, the *Celastrus orbiculatus* on the right, and the *Osmaronia cerasiflorus* on the lower right, which gives a false indication of spring by flowering in early February.

PLATE NO. 44
MIRROR BEHIND THE ALPINE HOUSE

One of the two large mirrors, used in the 'Big Brother' style to deter members of the public from making off with the small plantings of Campanulaceae, Iridaceae, and Ericaceae.

PLATE NO. 45
CART IN SNOW

This scene was found in 1985 along the path south of the Main Gates, towards the Ferneries. It is a barrow of older design, used by the gardeners to move many of the new seedlings around the Gardens.

PLATE NO. 46
BLACK PINE WITH DAFFODILS

This *Pinus nigra*, planted in 1814, now grows so high that it can be seen from outside the Main Gates.

PLATE NO. 47
DRY TROPICAL WING, PRINCESS OF WALES CONSERVATORY

The plants in this section grow naturally in the dry desert and semi-desert conditions that exist over 20% of the world's land surface. As well as the better-known cacti, examples include the exotic Mexican *Nolina recurvata* with fernlike fronds, shown here on the right of the picture.

PLATE NO. 48
WISTERIA CAGE

This round iron framework for the Wisteria growing on it stands on the site of the original Great Stove at Kew, which was designed by Chambers for Princess Augusta and was the largest hothouse in Britain at the time.

PLATE NO. 49
ARCHES, TEMPERATE HOUSE

The south-west corner of the walkway around the Temperate House is dazzling in the summer, since all of the ironwork is painted white. Through the tall windows is the roof of the Australian House.

PLATE NO. 50
RHAMNUS ALATERNUS ARGENTEOVARIEGATA, QUEEN'S GARDEN

The whole middle area of the Queen's Garden is covered by small, regular cobblestones. They are set off quite nicely here by this *Rhamnus alaternus*.

PLATE NO. 51
THE AROID HOUSE

Designed by John Nash in 1825, this was the first Architectural Conservatory of its day, and was moved in 1836 from the newly rebuilt Buckingham Palace, at the request of William IV. It was modified later by Sir Jeffrey Wyatville, but still retains its stone north wall.

PLATE NO. 52
THE CONSERVATION AREA

Roped off from the path to the west of Queen Charlotte's cottage is an area that was given to Kew Gardens by Queen Victoria as a Diamond Jubilee gift in 1897, with the condition that it be kept for posterity as a natural wilderness.

This picture shows wild grasses growing from a dip in the ground in the winter of 1986.

PLATE NO. 53
STATUE OF DAVID

The marble statue of David in the south-west corner

of the Temperate House is a 19th-century copy of the bronze figure by Donatello which was made around 1440 and originally stood in the courtyard of the Medici Palace in Florence.

PLATE NO. 54
LION GATE WALK

This part of the path between Lion Gate and the Palm House is north of the Heath Garden and contains some lovely examples of hickory and walnut trees.

PLATE NO. 55
EAST DOOR, TEMPERATE HOUSE

The Temperate House was designed by Decimus Burton and when completed, in 1899, after thirty-nine years of construction, was the largest glasshouse of its kind. Renovation, finished in 1981, included moving the four original boilers to the nearby stable yard. In summertime the four large doors at the east and west entrances are opened to assist ventilation.

PLATE NO. 56
PAN, QUEEN'S GARDEN

The middle statue of the five at the bottom of the Queen's Garden appropriately shows the horned god Pan, the Greek spirit of the natural world.

PLATE NO. 57
PRIVATE DOOR

There are a number of doors and gates marked PRIVATE along the road from the Main Gates to the Wood Museum. Most, like this one, go to the gardens of the old houses on this side of Kew Green, although to the right of this one is another door leading to a nursery.

PLATE NO. 58
HORNBEAMS IN WINTER, QUEEN'S GARDEN

The bark of these trees turn a lovely shade of green which is most noticeable in winter against the snow. This view is looking north towards the river, the opposite view to Plate No. 9.

PLATE NO. 59
SWAMP CYPRESS, PALM HOUSE POND

This large cypress is found at the side of the Pond. The impressive statue of Hercules slaying a sea serpent can be seen in the middle of the Pond.

PLATE NO. 60
MAIN GATES

These gates were designed by Decimus Burton, and erected in 1848 to the west of the former entrance.

The former gates had, mounted on either pillar, a lion and a unicorn. These animals have been moved to their own gates on Kew Road, although only Lion Gate is opened to the public.

PLATE NO. 61
CRATAEGUS MONOGYNA

The planting date for this hawthorn is not listed on the label, but one imagines it having witnessed palace life for many years. It not only requires a crutch for support, but the inside of the entire trunk at ground level is hollow.

PLATE NO. 62
TEMPLE OF AEOLUS

Built in 1760 by Sir William Chambers and redesigned by Decimus Burton in 1845, this lovely temple stands on an artificial hill by the Pond. It originally housed a revolving seat which gave sitters a 360-degree view of the gardens.

PLATE NO. 63
MANURE IN STABLE YARD

In the stable yard which is south of the Lake several tons of farm manure are stored for mulching plants against winter frost. The process of composting these huge piles includes water sprinklers which keep the moisture at the right level.

PLATE NO. 64
RHOPALOSTYLIS BAUERI, TEMPERATE HOUSE

This palm-like bush in the north-east corner of the Temperate House is indigenous to Norfolk Island.

PLATE NO. 65
THE ICE HOUSE

Built into the side of a hill, the Ice House is thought to have been built in the late 18th century. Ice was considered to be a great luxury at this time. Taken from several of the ponds that once existed between the Palm House and the river, the ice was used to cool drinks and keep food fresh.

The Ice House was restored in 1982, but is not usually open to the public.

PLATE NO. 66
TEMPERATE HOUSE THROUGH CEDARS

The landscaping of these cedars creates a small vista east/west between the Marianne North Gallery and the Temperate House.

PLATE NO. 67
GREEK URN, BROAD WALK CIRCLE

This is the larger of the two Circles, found on the south side of the Broad Walk. Beneath the Urn are planted a circle of *Canna indica*, *Artemisia arborescens*, and *Iresine lindenii*.

PLATE NO. 68
WOODCHIPS NEAR LION GATE

Another pile of mulching material was stored temporarily by the path west of Lion Gate. This is a collection of woodchips, and may have come from Kew's portable 'tree-eating' machine that reduces the largest tree to small and useful woodchips.

PLATE NO. 69
THROUGH THE MAIN GATES

The gold, scrolled letters at the top of the gates show Queen Victoria's monogram, and the two crests bear the royal coat of arms.

Through the years, the number of visitors coming to Kew Gardens has fluctuated enormously. In 1841, there were 9,714; in 1865, above 500,000; in 1908, W.J. Bean, the assistant curator, quoted nearly 3 million! The latest figure (1987) shows the number down to something over 1.5 million people.

PLATE NO. 70
DRINKING FOUNTAIN, ORANGERY

Situated· at the west end of the Orangery, this is probably the most used drinking fountain in the Gardens, and one of the nine marked on the official map.

  The fountain is a good example of the symbols of myth and legend that were so popular with the Victorians, and the wreathed and bearded head from whose mouth the water issues is probably the face of Hermes, messenger to the Gods.

PLATE NO. 71
MEDITERRANEAN WING, TEMPERATE HOUSE

The climber growing down the right-hand pillar is *Smilax aspera*, and the small tree in the background is an olive (*Olea europaea*) from the Balearic Islands.

PLATE NO. 72
EDWARD VII GATE, DUKE'S GARDEN

This is one of the two entrances to the Duke's Garden, and has the gold monogram of Edward VII. The tree on the left is an Asian *Buddleia crispa*, and the large tree beyond the gate is an Italian Lombardy poplar.

PLATE NO. 73
VIEW FROM TEMPERATE HOUSE

The vista looks west from the Temperate House steps towards Kew Road. This bench is the same as the one in Plate No. 66, but viewed from the opposite direction.

PLATE NO. 74
CIBOTIUM GLAUCUM, TEMPERATE HOUSE

A large fern indigenous to Hawaii, it grows here next to the waterfall in the middle of the Temperate House, where the sweep of the leaves offer a more impressive cascade than the waterfall itself.

PLATE NO. 75
BENCH IN SNOW, WINTER 1985

Just beyond the Aroid House on the first Broad Walk, this combination of bench and tree (*Pinus nigra*) is just one of the textural compositions found throughout the Gardens. In the background are the building materials on the site of the new Administration Building, east of the Palace, due for completion in 1988.

PLATE NO. 76
STAIRCASE INSIDE THE PAGODA

This is the original wooden staircase inside the Pagoda, which rises through ten floors to the observation room at the top. The staircase is the same size throughout the building, growing larger in ratio to the ten levels, which grow progressively smaller in diameter.

  The inside is due for redecoration, but the structure of the building is as sound as when it was built in 1691.

PLATE NO. 77
THE FARTHEST PLACE

At the south-west corner of the conservation area is the corner of Kew that is the farthest distance from the Main Gates. It borders on the Thames and the Richmond Park Golf Course.

  Although long since bricked over, this is the site of a very old entrance, called the King's Steps Gate, which was used from Windsor as a ferry landing point.

WAKEHURST PLACE

PLATE NO. 78
VIEW AT 'KODAK CORNER'

This spot was dubbed 'Kodak Corner' by the Wakehurst staff who found that more visitors took pictures of this view than any other place in the Garden. On the right are a Californian redwood, a Norwegian spruce, and a Spring sycamore in front, and on the left of the Mansion is a European birch with a large lime tree behind. In the Pond are a mixture of waterlilies including *Nuphar lutea*, the 'Brandy Bottle'.

PLATE NO. 79
ASH GROVE BY THE LAKE

Five young ash trees (*Fraxinus excelsior*) grow next to the lake at the Horsebridge Woods end. The photograph was taken in early spring 1987, so the groundcover is sparse.

PLATE NO. 80
ROCK WALK

The almost velvet appearance of the sandstone at this part of the Rock Walk is due to the fine moss growing over the stone. The path here is quite wide, but other parts have a much narrower path, which is not easily negotiated in wet or rainy weather.

PLATE NO. 81
SUNDIAL IN CARRIAGE RING

Between 1697 and the final removal in 1848 of the two main wings, many alterations were made to the Mansion. This stable block was made of the same sandstone and finished in 1727. In front of it is a large weeping silver lime (*Tilia petiolaris*), which is a tree of unknown origin.

PLATE NO. 82
MONKS IN DINING ROOM

These two monks on either side of the fireplace in the dining room are part of a later addition of panelling. The monks and the mantelpiece were probably imported from two different places.

PLATE NO. 83
BENCH AT 'KODAK CORNER'

This is probably the favourite bench at Wakehurst, considering the view back over the Pond toward the Mansion, and is one of dozens of benches throughout both Kew and Wakehurst which have been given in memory of deceased relatives or friends.

PLATE NO. 84
SWAMP CYPRESS, WESTWOOD LAKE

Taken in the early spring of 1986 before the green growth by the edge of the Lake obscured the view, this photograph shows the unusual choice of location by *Taxodium distichum* – almost as though it can't decide whether to be a land based or an aquatic tree.

PLATE NO. 85
APPROACH TO ROCK WALK

Where Horsebridge Woods meet the sandstone cliffs of the Rock Walk, the landscape begins to rise more steeply on one side. On the left can be seen young trees within fences, built to protect the branches from animals.

PLATE NO. 86
ARCHWAY TO THE PLEASAUNCE

Separating the Sir Henry Price Garden from the older Pleasaunce is a redesigned wall in a meadow-brick style. Little has been changed in these two Gardens, apart from narrowing the yew hedge, which the Boord family planted in 1890, and the statue of the boy, which in 1986 was bought to replace a statue of another boy strangling a swan.

PLATE NO. 87
WESTWOOD VALLEY

In the distance a bonfire burns. It is on this side of the Slips that one can see a specimen of the deciduous conifer, the golden larch (*Pseudolarix amabilis*), native to China, which is rare in cultivation and the only member of its genus.

The valley is planted with a number of trees and shrubs, among them some healthy magnolias which flower in early summer.

PLATE NO. 88
BRIDGE OVER ROCK WALK

There is a large European larch (*Larix decidua*) next to the small wooden bridge that runs over a storm ditch.

PLATE NO. 89
PACKHORSE BRIDGE, WATER GARDEN

Built about ten years ago by Reginald Childs, this simple bridge of local stone was built in the traditional packhorse style, and is on one of several paths that run through the water garden.

PLATE NO. 90
ROOTS AT ROCK WALK

The roots spanning the gap in the sandstone outcrops show how delicately the trees here have their hold on the soil.

The raised rock in the foreground is popular for sliding down, one visitor having inscribed the date of his visit (1985).

PLATE NO. 91
LAWSON CYPRESS

This tall blue cypress (*Chamaecyparis lawsoniana*) grows in the Pinetum, and is a blue form of evergreen, probably 'Glauca'.

PLATE NO. 92
WALNUT TREE, BLOOMER'S VALLEY

When felled in a storm, this walnut tree was left for aesthetic reasons and because it was still growing. The house in the background is a pump house that feeds the Bethlehem Woods nursery from a natural spring.

PLATE NO. 93
INSIDE SOUTH DOOR, WAKEHURST MANSION

Close inspection of the stone archway reveals some interesting graffiti: JOHИ ARИOLD 1665. One of

the policemen in the Gardens suggests that the responsible party may well have been a Canadian soldier billetted in the Mansion during the Second World War.

PLATE NO. 94
THE GAZEBO

There are five shelters at Wakehurst (the same number as at Kew), and they are placed where they offer the best views of the Gardens. This one is tucked away to the east of Mansion Pond, and shows a lovely view back across the Pond to the Mansion.

PLATE NO. 95
YEW HEDGE AT THE PLEASAUNCE

Another photograph of the Pleasaunce (see Plate No. 86) showing the sculpted yew hedge and the fountain in the middle of this formal garden.

PLATE NO. 96
BEECH TREE ON ROCK WALK

This beech is one of several trees that grow from the natural outcrop of sandstone surrounding the farmland in the middle of the Wakehurst estate.

The trees are mostly of beech and oak and when they appear, like this one, to issue directly from the rock itself, their growth seems to be largely unimpaired.

PLATE NO. 97
STEPS SOUTH OF THE MANSION

The lawn behind these original steps shows where the two southern wings of the Mansion were removed over a hundred years ago. Until then, and since it was built in 1590, it was a typical E-shaped Elizabethan mansion.

PLATE NO. 98
BIRD HIDE, LODER VALLEY

Looking like a blasted tree until close inspection, this hollow trunk is one of at least three bird hides for enthusiasts. This one is the most impressive, being just next to the reservoir.

PLATE NO. 99
ARDINGLY RESERVOIR

Separating Ardingly from Balcombe (where most
of the reservoir is situated) is a small causeway that
was built to resite a two-lane road. The fence going
into the water is a boundary line between the
reserve and Brook cottage.

PLATE NO. 100
PLATT'S BRIDGE, ARDINGLY
RESERVOIR

This bridge marks the northern boundary of the
Loder Valley Reserve, and had to be built to main-
tain a public footpath from the Gardener's Arms
(on the B2028) to the Balcombe Ridge. The rails
were built with tiny dovetail joins along the sides,
which can be seen by close inspection.

  The Loder Valley reserve, situated south-west of
Wakehurst Place is called 'A Botanical Reserve for
Wealden Vegetation' and since 1977 has been a
natural conservation area. To protect the wildlife,
the area is open strictly by appointment with the
Administrator at Wakehurst and the reserve even
has a full-time Warden, sometimes armed with a
shotgun against poachers.